The Freedom Permit

Creating A Vision of Discipleship For Your Senior's Last Year in High School

2nd Edition

Tommy McGregor

TABLE OF CONTENTS

How To Use This Book

This book is for parents of high school seniors and is a resource to help those parents create a vision for how to best utilize their child's last year at home before graduation. Why is that important? Well, if you are a parent of a soon-to-be graduating senior, you already know the answer to that question. But, for the sake of clarity, it is important because most teenagers leave home unprepared for the challenges that life will provide them at the next stage. That new stage might be at a four-year college or university, a junior college, the military, or in the work force. Whatever their path, life will not be the same for these young adults who are out in the world for the first time on their own.

(NOTE: Just like in my other books and writings, I will use the word "college" because that is where most students I work with go after high school. If your child is going to another place mentioned above, simply make the change in your mind as you read. The concepts of The Freedom Permit will work with any situation, post-high school).

This book will give you, the parent, a vision to cast, a plan to make, and a starting point to begin. The concept of this book is simple: use this last year to equip your child with the tools needed to thrive at the next level. I am not giving you a completed plan, but rather, I am giving you a frame in which to build a plan that is specific for your child. You may have a year or just a few months. You know how much time you have and so I recommend that you use it wisely.

Each parent will use this material differently; therefore, I suggest that you take the time to answer the questions and then think strategically about how this approach will help your child prepare for the next chapter of life. If you have questions about this material, please do not hesitate to contact me via email at tommy@thetransmission.org. I also want to direct you to TheTransMission website for an online library of content to help you in this process. The address www.thetransmission.org and you can read more about TheTransMission in the last section of this book. I pray that God will give you wisdom and discernment as you teach your child these life lessons this year through the Freedom Permit. Blessings to you on the journey!

Tommy McGregor
founder, TheTransMission

Chapter 1
Understanding The Transition

Each year, I meet parents who come up to me looking like a deer caught in the headlights. These parents all have two major things in common. One, they have a senior in high school. Two, they are beginning to feel afraid of the alluring transition that will take place sometime during that year. Based on the month in which I encounter these nervous parents, the headlight's reflection in the eyes of these "deer" parents gets brighter as the school calendar counts down. Recently, I met a dad who was only four days from moving his son into a college freshman dorm three hours from home. Let's just say that this transition was already attempting to swerve to avoid road kill.

Most of the parents that I meet in this situation do not feel like they have done enough to prepare their kids for life after high school. Unfortunately, a green light doesn't blink on once the child is fully prepared, as if he is a phone charging to full power. No parent has ever admitted to me that a bell sounded once a student has finally uploaded all the content and instruction she will need to make a healthy transition to adulthood. It comes down to faith, trust, and the belief that you have done the very best you can with the wisdom that God gave you.

Before we dive into the concept of the Freedom Permit, I think it is important to understand why this transition is so difficult for the students making it. The statistics suggest that between two-thirds and three-fourths of Christian teenagers graduate from high school and fail to continue growing and maturing in their faith in Christ within one year of that graduation. Is this because 65-75% of kids who grew up in church are ready to chuck that faith into the air along with the graduation cap? I don't think so. I know for myself, I had every intention to continue developing the faith that I held tightly to in high school, but yet I struggled with connecting. This is not to say that I did not have friends in college; I had hundreds of them, but none of them were willing or able to support me in my faith and keep me accountable for it.

Life is filled with many seasons and stages, all with transitions between them. When facing one of these transitions, we must prepare ourselves and begin to understand how we can continue living in that new setting of life. In my vast experience of dealing with teenagers in this transitional stage, I have found that the majority are simply not prepared. They have lived their entire life in the nest and, now that it is time to fly away, they do not know how.

Balancing In A New Current
Once in a media interview, someone asked me to sum up the struggles of this transition into one word. Even without putting more than a second of thought in it, I said "connecting." Think for a moment about the influences that your child has had throughout high school. For most Christian high school seniors, there have been up to four major spiritual influences in their lives: family, friends, church, and mentors. If a teenager comes from a family that modeled a life in Christ, then he was very fortunate and blessed. Secondly, if he had a church that has taught him how to walk in Christ, as well as a mentor, such as a youth pastor, teacher, or coach to help mold him, then he would most likely be a maturing follower of Christ by graduation time. Likewise, if a child also had Christian friends to lean on as they grew up together, that student would understand the value of accountability and community in her life. When a

student has these four influences, those relationships have helped to construct a spiritual infrastructure for that teenager during those years of growth. The problem is that few, if any, of these influences will follow that individual to college. The teen might have some of his high school friends go to the same college, but rarely does anyone take an entire friend base to the next level.

Even for those students who will be going to school in their hometown, living at home, and continuing to attend the same church, life will still be different.

By the time an individual, with these four influences intact, enters his senior year in high school, life often resembles someone flowing down the current of a river on an inner-tube. All an individual has to do in that moment is hang on and enjoy the ride. He knows where to go for discipleship, accountability, advice, fellowship, worship, serving opportunities, and overall community, because those relationships have long been established, allowing life to be fun and carefree. So, the logical assumption for many in this situation is that if they can continue to stay steady as they move on to college, then they will be fine. They remember how well they did in high school, floating down the river, and so they try to continue to do the same thing in college. What they don't factor in is that the currents in college flow differently than in high school. There is a stronger undertow. It is not that they can't do it, but they just have to understand how to do it differently. They must learn how to balance in the new current.

In the introduction of my book, *Lost in Transition*, I ask high school seniors and college freshmen a key question: *Are you as spiritually mature right now as you want to be on the day you graduate from college?* What I am really asking them is if they are willing to be 22 or 23 years old, facing life decisions that a young adult faces at that age (new job, serious relationships, first real paycheck, etc), with the faith maturity of a 17 or 18 year old? This is not only a possibility, but a default setting for most individuals of this age.

The Current State of Your High School Senior

As a student finally approaches his senior year in high school, they have spent almost all of their recollected life in school and at home, under the supervision of loving parents and teachers; but now that is about to change. With some nervousness and much excitement, they are preparing for a great leap into adulthood where they will have more freedom than ever before. For both parent and student, this is a stressful time of wrapping up one chapter of life and preparing for another.

At this point in the process, most seniors have at least narrowed it down as to where they are going to go to college. They have taken the tests and have done just about all that they can do academically to graduate. Many of them have actually "clocked-out" of high school (mentally, emotionally, and maybe even physically) already and are just going through the motions to make it to graduation. Parents are finding it harder to communicate to their senior and focus them on anything constructive as the student and the parent, even more than usual, find themselves on two separate wavelengths. While the parent wants to draw them in, the senior feels the need to pull apart. There are always exceptions to this, but for many the tensions at home are rising.

The typical mindset of a high school senior is an anomaly. They are physically here, living the regular day-to-day life of school, family, and church, but they are mentally there, daydreaming about life as a college student. Sometime in the first grade, a teacher probably told them what graduating class they were in. This seemed like a lifetime away, to you and to them, and yet that year is now approaching (if not already here). A student begins to look forward to her senior year around middle school and, each year, longs more and more for the moment of becoming the big man on campus. Then, once that moment finally comes, something strange happens. The longing is over, the time has arrived and the typical high school senior overlooks this year of seniority to gaze upon the beautiful pastures of college life. This is a condition commonly known as Senioritis.

What is Senioritis?
About this time every year, just as summer ends and the new school year begins, an intermittent sickness spreads throughout households of those anticipating graduation that year. Could it be a virus that only affects certain ages at specific times? Might it be brought on by transitional stress at the end of the high school years? Is it contagious and could it potentially become a pandemic? To these and other possible questions: Yes!

Senioritis begins sometime after the start of the college application process and has been known to linger through-out the summer months until the infected moves off to college. Common symptoms of Senioritis include a basic lack of desire to do anything productive at home or school and tiredness, even after a three-hour nap. According to my own observations, this energy deficiency seems to flare up when the affected is anywhere except in close proximity to other infected individuals in social settings. The reasons for this are unclear, but my own research has authenticated its claims. Other symptoms of senioritis can include, but are not limited to, an extreme lack of communication, inability to complete regular household responsibilities, and a decrease in concern for...anything.

For parents dealing with this condition at home, extreme patience is required. In my experience, the best treatment is prayer and large doses of ibuprofen, for the parent, not necessarily the senior. Parental caregivers have been known to get through this time by quoting such phrases like, "This too shall pass," "They will be gone soon," and various Psalms on suffering and deliverance.

Preparing For The Transition

There is an odd exchange that takes place in the life of a recent high school graduate the day he moves away to go to college or other post high school destinations of choice. The night before, he lives under his parents' roof, which incorporates everything from a curfew to a home-cooked meal. Then, literally, the next morning, he packs up and leaves behind all rules, standards, expectations, and protections that he deems unnecessary for the journey ahead. For the majority of teenagers, they blaze a new trail of identity that matches the land of opportunity visible on the next horizon. College is a very social place and students entering this new culture will feel the pressures to adapt to their new surroundings. Many decisions will be made that will weigh heavier on their future than ever before. The question is not, will this happen to your child, but rather, how will your child respond when it happens?

Questions:

1. Think for a moment about your transition to college (decisions, behaviors, relationships...). How do you want your child's experience to be same/different?

_____

_____

_____

_____

_____

_____

_____

_____

2. What is the mindset of your senior right now?

_____

_____

_____

_____

_____

_____

3. What are your fears about your child going to college next year?

_____

_____

_____

_____

_____

4. What are the three things you think they might struggle with the most in college?

_____

_____

_____

_____

_____

_____

5. What are some of the key points from this chapter that you will need to remember?

_____

_____

_____

_____

_____

_____

Chapter 2
The Freedom Permit

Do you remember the day you received your driver's license? I recall the morning I got mine. I had been dreaming of sitting behind the wheel for years, with nothing but freedom in my view. I knew that this was a monumental moment in my life. I was ready. I got to the test and passed it with flying colors. It was my 16th birthday, and all was right with the world.

I passed that driving test for one main reason. I had spent the past 364 days with what we call a driver's permit. This is a card that is issued to a person prior to earning a driver's license. A driver's permit represents a training period where the permitted learns how to handle the freedoms of driving an automobile, with Mom or Dad in the passenger seat. For me this was a year long process. My father and I would go to an empty parking lot and practice driving. I recall receiving instruction as if I was training to man the international space station. I never knew that when someone headed out on a quick errand that the process was so in-depth. As the months went on, I got better, though every time I did something wrong I was told that I had just hit an old lady crossing the street. The fact is I hit a lot of invisible pedestrians that year, but in the end, I learned how to safely drive a car. Since receiving my driver's license a few decades ago, I have developed the art of driving and built on to the skill that I learned that year of learning (and I haven't hit an invisible person since).

Issuing Another Kind of Permit

As you read this book, your child is in his last year of high school. Next year he will experience the most freedom he has ever had to date. For most teenagers, this is the largest dose of freedom that they have received since gaining the ability to drive. What if you, the parent, view this last year of high school as another permit year. Like with the driving permit, your child can spend this year learning how to handle life on his or her own, with you in the passenger seat. This is your opportunity to build on everything that you have ever taught them about life, faith, and responsibility. This will include many important conversations, a lot of very teachable moments, and a year's worth of memorable experiences that all help your freedom learner understand what it takes to live as a mature adult. It is time to issue a Freedom Permit.

Next Level Parenting

One very important component of this transition that is often overlooked is the fact that the parents go through a transition, too. Much attention is put on the student's transition to college, and rightfully so, but the parents must learn to transition as well.

The truth is a parent goes through many transitions as the child grows through the different stages of life. I would like to highlight five stages called the 5 C's of parenting. The first stage is that of the Caregiver. This is the first stage a parent begins with as a baby is born and grows from infant to toddler. The next stage is that of the Cop. The Cop is raising a child from toddler to pre-schooler and into early grade school as the parent teaches the rules of authority and how to obey. The third role is commonly referred to as the Coach.

Depending on the maturity level of the child, this stage will hope- fully begin in the early teenage years. The Coach gets to train and instruct the child on life. I have seen this coaching relationship between the parent and child work very well, and I have also seen it misconnect. The fourth stage is the one that you should either already be in with your senior or hoping to move into this year. This is the role of the Counselor. A Counselor is one who asks questions and has conversations. The Counselor is still in authority but more in a role of reinforcing on a foundation of learning rather than building from scratch. This level can start with an older teenager and continues through the first year or two of college. A healthy Counselor relationship is based on trust, respect, and openness. The final stage is Collaborator. This is an adult to adult relationship where the parent and son/ daughter work together and teach each other through their relationship.

An important question to ask yourself is, "Where are you with your high school senior?" You might find that you are still in the Coach stage with occasional signs of the Cop slipping in on weekends. My hope is that you see evidence of the Counselor in your relationship, or you have a goal to be heading more in that direction this year. I think this is important to this process because an older teenager thinks of himself as approaching adulthood. He wants more freedom and is often open to the responsibilities that come with it. Furthermore, he desires such respect from his parents, even if he has not yet earned it. Entering into the Counselor stage with him might give him the appreciation he needs and draw you closer in relationship. The truth is, the Freedom Permit will require a Pre-Counselor level of communication to be effective. My challenge is that you try hard to work to that end, even if it means giving-in a little more than you are comfortable with giving at first.

The Four Parts of the Freedom Permit
The Freedom Permit is only a concept. It is nothing more than a creative way for me to tell parents that I see dramatic deficiencies in college kids today, and there needs to be an intentional focus put on the preparation for this transition to life after high school.

The Freedom Permit has four parts: Spiritual Development, Life Management, Social Behaviors, and Goal Setting. These four categories represent the deficiencies that I see among college students attempting to navigate through life away from home. Many college students, who grew up in a church, leave home and never replace that influence of community, worship, and discipleship. Often, students who were involved in small group Bible studies in high school go off to college and never feel the void to find another group for accountability. All college students leave home with the expectation to manage time and money effectively enough to make it to class on time and have food to eat when they get hungry. College life forces students to make decisions on their own that will affect them socially, academically, physically, emotionally, and spiritually. Spending this last year focusing on these four areas will help kids understand the world they are about to enter and begin to know how to live in it.

Now I would like to give you five suggestions as you prepare for this senior year with your child. These five things will help you better usher in the Freedom Permit as well as help you combat the effects of Senioritis.

1. Begin With A Flow of Open Communication
Before you begin the process of discipling your senior, I want to re-emphasize the importance of communication. It is important to open up the flow of conversation between you and your graduating senior about their excitements, fears, concerns, and anticipations of college. One of the

biggest implementations of the Freedom Permit is having conversations often with your child. As Moses instructs parents in Deuteronomy 6:6-8, parents are to talk about the commands of God, "when you sit at home and when you walk along the road, when you lie down and when you get up." For some, this will be natural because the channels of conversation in the family are always open and honest, but for others this may not be the case. Living with a teenager is sometimes like living with a snake; you are never sure if you will get a passive pet or a venomous viper. Often times, by a student's senior year, the waves of conversation are shutting down making it difficult to instruct, much less disciple. Allow them to share their thoughts with you so that they know you are interested. Many teenagers wrongfully think that parents are not interested in hearing their point of view. Kids can become so accustomed to being told what to do during the Cop and Coach phase that they begin to doubt the existence of a Counselor or Collaborator stage. Open communication, without constant instruction, will be a relationship builder.

2. Learn To Pray With Your Children

You, most likely, already pray for your children, but do you pray with them and over them? If not, your kids may never know that you constantly pray for them unless they hear you pray for them. There is a power surge that rushes through you when you know someone is praying specifically for you. This will help develop the needed trust and openness that the Freedom Permit requires. If this is odd or difficult for you, then work up to it. Tell them one day that you are praying for them. Then pray for them when you might already be praying out loud, at dinner for example. Then ask them if you can pray over them. Soon it will be more natural. Throughout this process, it is a good thing if your family sees a change in you. Let them know that things are different now, and everyone will be stronger because of it.

3. Consider Giving Them A Little More Freedom
Within a year, your college freshman will have virtually unlimited freedom. Give them a little more freedom now to see how they handle it. Not only will this gesture be appreciated, but it can be leveraged as a teaching point as the year goes on. This should obviously be a gradual thing, but a little later curfew or extra privilege will go a long way to help them not feel so "trapped" in their senior year, and it will help prepare them for the year after.

4. Give Them Something To Do To Fill Their Time, Outside Of School. Remember, many seniors are coasting down a river on a tube during this last year of high school. As Senioritis creeps in they will long for lazy afternoons and weekends to pass the time. Help them get involved in something useful. They could get a job or intern/shadow someone in a field that they are interested in. This will allow them to focus on something related to the major that they will pursue in college. They could serve and develop a passion for a cause larger than themselves. They could volunteer or work to make extra money for college. Too much spare time and Senioritis are very bad when mixed together.

5. Prepare Yourself For The Christmas Reality Check
A few years ago, I spoke to one-half of the senior class at a Christian high school in November. One of the questions that I asked to the students was, "Do you feel like your parents are letting out the rope of freedom a little or drawing you in tighter?" The over- whelming answer was that the parents were in fact giving them some slack in the rope. Two months later, in January, I spoke to the other half of the senior class of the same school. When I asked the same question, I got the opposite answer. These seniors complained that they started out with more slack but were feeling the tug harder and harder now from their parents. The conclusion I discovered was that something happens over Christmas break with many parents of seniors. I call it

the Christmas Reality Check. The tree is decorated and the presents are filling in below. The Christmas cards have been mailed out and the family traditions are in full swing. Then it happens. Mom and Dad realize that next year will be different. Next Christmas, at least one child will have to come home to celebrate the holidays. Things will never be as they have always been. From that moment on, the rope tension begins to tighten. Kids feel this right away, and it can cause them to wish that the remaining days at home could pass even faster. Be prepared for feelings like this and try really hard not to let them see you sweat it.

Questions:

1. Think about each of the five stages of parenting and what you have learned about your child throughout that journey? Which stage do you think you thrive more in and which do you feel your child learns more in?

_____

_____

_____

_____

_____

_____

_____

2. How would you characterize your child's level of
   independence and how might that affect this senior
   year?

_____

_____

_____

_____

_____

_____

_____

3. Reflect back on the list of five things at the end of
   this section. How can you put those five
   suggestions into practice to ease the tension of the
   Senior Year?

_____

_____

_____

_____

_____

_____

_____

_____

_____

_____

4. How do you think this senior year will change your
   relationship with your child as you help guide him or her
   through the Freedom Permit?

_____

_____

_____

_____

_____

_____

_____

5. What are some of the key points from this chapter that
   you will need to remember?

_____

_____

_____

_____

_____

_____

_____

_____

Chapter 3
Spiritual Development

I have always felt that the overall health of our life is contingent on the condition of our soul, meaning that if we are healthy spiritually then we will become healthy in all other aspects of life. We find this idea supported in verses like Mark 6:33 where Jesus said, "Seek first his kingdom and his righteousness, and all these things will be given to you as well." We know from John 15:5 that we are to connect to Christ as a vine connects to a branch because in Christ we can bear fruit and without him we can do nothing.

One of the biggest factors that I have seen in students who struggle with this transition is that they are what the apostle Paul called infants in Christ (1 Corinthians 3:1). Even though they grew up in church and around faith throughout life, they are still feeding on milk, rather than solid food. In 1 Corinthians 13:11 it says, "When I was a child, I talked like a child, I thought like a child, I reasoned like a child. When I became a man, I put the ways of childhood behind me". Now is the time for this to happen spiritually for your high school senior. Regardless of how mature you child may be, it is time to grow deeper so that he will learn to "grasp how wide and long and high and deep is the love of Christ, and to know this love that surpasses knowledge—that (they) may be filled to the measure of all the fullness of God." (Ephesians 3:18-19).

As you spend this year developing the faith of your teenager, I suggest that you take it slow and steady. First, you will need to evaluate the maturity of your child's faith. Is your child following Jesus or just going through the motions? Pulling in your pastor or a mentor to help you determine this might be helpful. As with all of these categories, active conversations are key. Begin to ask your child faith questions. Ask them to say the prayer at dinner tonight and see if you think they are talking to a Father that they truly know or a Being that is distant and foreign. Ask your child about certain verses and see if they know the verse and what it means. Such prodding will help you understand where your child is on the journey and where to start.

Starting From Scratch

It is reasonable to think that some parents will need to start this process from scratch because they are not used to having spiritual conversations in the home. If this is the case, I suggest that you begin with prayer. First, pray for the courage and strength to begin this process, and then involve your child in those prayers. Chances are you will need to sit down with your child and discuss that, though these spiritual conversations may seem strange and foreign at first, they are important and necessary from this point forward. Prepare to be vulnerable as you admit fault in not focusing more on spiritual development in the home in the past. Enjoy the process of growing together as you pray, read Scripture, and talk together about who Jesus is and who you both are in Christ. Go to church together, serve in missions together, and encourage your child to become surrounded with other believers in community. If you had to forgo focusing on the other three components of this plan to center on this first one, it would still be worth it in the end. As 1 Timothy 4:15 says, "Take pains with these things; be absorbed in them, so that your progress will be evident to all."

Working The Plan
As with all of the categories of this plan, I will break them up into three parts: Conversations, Studies, and Actions. For Spiritual Development, each of these pieces is important to the overall growth of your child this year.

Spiritual Conversations: In the theme of Moses' instruction to talk about faith daily in Deuteronomy 6, the more this becomes a topic of conversation, the more it will be in the mind and heart of the family. Here are ten questions that you might consider asking your child as you "sit at home and when you walk along the road, when you lie down and when you get up;" as well as when you drive, eat, go to the store, church, and on trips together:

• *What have been some of the most important 'God moments' of your life?*

• *When have you grown the most in your faith since you became a Christian?*

• *If you could come up with a verse that serves as a mantra or life verse, what would it be and why?*

• *What has God been teaching you this past year?*

• *How would you describe your faith journey (testimony) to this point in your life?*

• *Who have been some of the biggest spiritual influences in your life and why?*

• *What are a few of the main lessons of faith that you have learned from these influences?*

- *What does it mean to be the Light of the World (see Matt 5:14)?*

- *What have been the catalysts for your growth in Christ and how will that change after you start college?*

- *What are five things that you have learned about yourself in high school, and how will recognizing those five things help you as you start college?*

For more questions in this and other transition related topics, look at the 53 questions posted in the Student Resource Library on TheTransMission website (www.thetransmission.org).

Spiritual Studies: Along with faith challenging questions, you should disciple your child this year with spiritual studies in God's Word. In my experience, many young believers do not really know what the Bible says and what it means to follow Jesus. So, how do you help a high schooler develop faith through study? As I tell student pastors in ministry training settings, take everything that you have taught them about faith over the years and apply it to a life in college. This will obviously vary from person to person, but focusing on the basics of faith is a good start. Prayer, worship, community, serving, and reading the Word are good places to begin. I would suggest a family Bible Study as you learn and grow together. Then, as you talk about the Church as the Body of Christ, find verses in the Bible about the Church and talk about your church. The more of an appreciation and love that your teenager has for church the more he will desire to connect to a new faith community in college. Talk about how to find a church and why it is important to be connected with other believers in college. This is the central issue for why the transition is so difficult for so many. As you spend the year in study and discipleship, go as deep as your child can go, always applying Biblical truth to the setting of life in college.

Spiritual Action: In James 2:14 we learn that faith must be followed by action. This last year of high school is a great opportunity for your child to put hands and feet on faith and learn what it means to serve. Again, in the Student Resource Library, I have an article called "Take The 25:40 Challenge". This would be a great activity for your senior to take on this year as it will challenge him or her to give to the least of these. A few ideas that can be done this year might be:

- going to the local homeless shelter on weekends and serving a meal.
- planning a mission trip as a senior trip or vacation to a far away location.
- serving at church in a leadership or volunteer role.
- looking for opportunities to teach younger kids about the Bible.
- having your child start a journal to record how she sees God working.
- learning what it means to work, earn money, and then give that money to those in need.

Challenge your child to be creative and fill this last year at home with spiritual actions that will support and build his faith in Christ. As the year progresses, the conversations, studies, and actions should get more specific and college transition related. Here are three late spring/early summer topics to focus on that pertain to faith and college:

1. **Help Your Child Develop a Personal Mission Statement.** Let them know that a mis-sion statement is a declaration that a business uses to tell the world who they are. A personal mission statement will do the same thing for an individual. For more on this, see the article in the Student Resource Library as well as the section in my book *Lost in Transition* about mission statements.

2. **Help Them Have A Connection Plan.** Once your child leaves for college, he will be on his own. It is crucial that

he connects well in the first few days/weeks of college. Freshmen need to find friends that will encourage them in their faith as well as groups that will help them continue to grow spiritually and mature. This usually does not happen automatically. Your child needs a plan, and you can help him by talking through it.

3. **Help Them Identify The Type of Church They Would Best Fit Into**. Most high school students have not ever had to look for a church by themselves. Usually, teenagers go to the church their parents attend or one where some friends go. Yet, if a student is going to replace that influence in college, he will need to understand the qualities to look for in a new church and have the confidence to jump into a new setting, feet first. A first step might be to get online and find some church options. Then, consider traveling together as a family to visit some of those churches when you do a college visit. Lastly, talk through the options and ask questions. Incoming freshman should have an idea of where they want to visit before moving to college.

Just as your child was once in training to be a driver, now he is learning how to handle the responsibility of life on his own. This process starts at the core with faith. When our relationship in Christ is growing, all other aspects of life will grow too. Once you begin to lead the Faith Development piece of this plan, the next one to begin looking at is Life Management.

Questions

1. How would you describe your child's spiritual level of maturity over the past few years?

_____

_____

_____

_____

_____

_____

_____

2. What have been some of the main factors to the growth or lack of growth that you have noticed in your child?

_____

_____

_____

_____

_____

_____

_____

3. How do you see that maturity level changing over to next year in college?

_____

_____

_____

_____

_____

_____

_____

4. Describe your fears &/or excitements about having spiritual conversations with your child this year? How will you plan to introduce this process?

_____

_____

_____

_____

_____

_____

_____

5. What are some of the key points from this chapter that you will need to remember?

_____

_____

_____

_____

_____

_____

_____

_____

Chapter 4
Life Management

I remember the day I stood over the washer and dryer at my childhood home as my mother taught me how to wash my own clothes. This was not a skill that I had needed to learn prior to going to college, so I was getting washing instructions a few weeks after graduation. When I got to college, I remember having to call home because the buttons on the community washers were different, but I quickly got it and started washing my own clothes.

There are so many things that kids take for granted while living at home that they will need to learn before moving away. Practically, every basic skill that is currently done for them now will need to be taught before the transition begins. I remember after my wife and I got engaged that she invited me over to her parent's house for dinner because she was cooking. She had cooked some growing up, but as with any typical 21 year-old, her personal recipe book was thin. To prepare her to be the primary cook for our new family, she decided that she would cook one meal a week for their family. Over the period of our year-long engagement, my future wife learned how to prepare meals of every kind, a fact that I am still very thankful for today. In the same way, teaching your senior to do these things and then allowing them to practice those skills while still at home is the process of preparing for Life Management.

When I was a kid, we had a family joke that the Bible said, "The Lord helps those who help themselves." I think I remember the reference being in 2 Philistines. My father would make this statement when I was not being personally responsible for myself. Even though it was always said in a joking manner, I learned that I needed to carry my weight in our family and not depend on others out of laziness. This is an important lesson to learn, while still at home, before a student moves away from the responsible accountability of parents.

Defining Life Management

So, what am I referring to when I use the term, Life Management? Yes, you guessed it: it is learning how to manage your day to day life. This is the process of preparing them to manage all of the aspects of life that previously have been managed or co-managed by parents & other adults. I think we all agree that we want to raise functional members of society who know how to take care of themselves, remembering that even everyday tasks are not automatically understood by someone who has never had to do them before.

When my wife and I got married, we moved half way across the country for me to start a new ministry job. One day after settling into our new community, my wife said that she was going to run a few errands. I had a couple of checks that needed to be deposited, and I knew that she would be driving past our local bank. When I asked her to make the deposit for me, she informed me that she had never done that before. She had the look of fear on her face as she asked about what to say at the drive-up window and how to make the deposit transaction. I was shocked because this task was second nature to me. As it turned out, her father had always made deposits for her. Their family bank was close to his work; and therefore, this was an easy errand for him to do for the entire family. We ended up taking the deposit to the bank together that day, so she could see how it was done. I have heard of college-aged girls who have never had to pump gas before and guys who did not know how to iron a shirt. This might sound silly to you and me who have done these things for years, but if you have never done these simple tasks, you have to learn how.

Working The Plan
Teaching life skills to your teenagers should be easy in theory. You can probably come up with a long list of things that they need to learn to do on their own. Make a list and then teach those tasks to them, remembering the importance of learning the responsibility and then practicing the responsibility until they learn the trait. Once again, lets look at this in the three categories of Conversations, Studies, and Actions.

Life Management Conversations: This process begins with thinking about the day-to-day activities you do for your child. Ask them, "When you are in college, what will you eat for breakfast in the morning?" When they say that they might skip breakfast, remind them about the importance of starting the day with protein and nourishment. Have them talk you through the process of completing certain tasks like going to the bank, changing a tire, washing and drying clothes, resetting the internet modem, and checking the smoke detectors. As you think of personal responsibilities that your child may not yet know, ask them about it and be prepared to instruct them on how it is done.

Life Management Studies: For some tasks, more study will be involved. It might be that the steps are too in depth for conversation only, or it includes something that you your- self are not sure how to properly explain. I mentioned changing a tire. This is something that every driver needs to know in case it happens without help. You may not feel like you can teach this well, so you either find someone else who can or you study it together. As you probably know, there is a Youtube video for everything these days. Find a video teaching how to change a tire and watch it. Then it is time to practice.

Life Management Actions. Practice makes perfect, they say, and most people learn best by doing. Once you have talked about it and learned about it, it is time to actually do it. Have your senior be the one in the family who goes to the bank to make deposits, or pumps the gas for your car, or shops and then cooks a meal each week for the family. This will help your student learn new skills and be fun as it will help the him stay involved in the day to day family activities.

The King and Queen of Life Management

So far we have talked about daily responsibilities that your child will need to develop, but now we need to focus on the two most important life management issues of them all: Time & Money. The typical teenager will go through high school never needing to totally manage either of these two important responsibilities. Mom wakes him up in the morning, keeps up with his dentist appointments, and stands over him to confirm that he has done all of his homework. Dad puts money in her checking account, reconciles the statement, and keeps track of the balance so that she doesn't get charged an overdraft fee. To a child, these responsibilities happen automatically without much concern from the teenager. But if these tasks are not learned before the student is on his own, the stress of irresponsibility will be lurking just around the corner. A college student will need to instantly become responsible for getting up for class, having assignments ready, and getting to bed at a good time to prepare for the next day. Likewise, most college freshmen are inexperienced in knowing how to manage money. Whether you give them a debit card, allowance, or they get a part-time job, they will be more on their own financially than ever before. Below are a few tips in handling these two management giants.

Teaching Time Management: There is no better way to teach time management other than to practice it, and practicing time management is best done when there is still a safety net in place to catch them when they fall. I suggest starting out by making them keep a calendar of personal and family events. This is so much easier than it once was with smartphones and syncing calendar apps for the computer. You could actually monitor their calendar in real time by using the same user account online. Require them to get up for school every morning on their own, with the understanding that if you have to wake them up, you might do so with a cup of cold water. If they have a doctor's appointment, put it on them to get there, and if they miss it, make them responsible for rescheduling. Next year, if they miss an appointment with an advisor, that is exactly what will have to happen. Talk to them about the necessary daily responsibilities they will need to schedule (eating, exercising, quiet time, rest, studying) and have them fill out a printable weekly schedule that includes every item. The goal is to have them personally responsible for their time before they move away to college.

Teaching Money Management: A recent survey showed that the average college student acquires $3000 worth of credit card debt while in school. This debt is not made up of student loans or family debt, but rather expenses that the student racks up while living at college. Even though some of that could be emergency related expenses, we know that most of it is probably due to mismanagement of personal funds. Students need to have an idea of how much money they will have available to them whether it be in the form of an allowance or bills being paid directly by the parents. They need to understand how to budget this money along with money they may earn themselves. Yet, not understanding how to handle that money or how easily accessible credit

38

cards are for broke students, debt can begin to accumulate even before the individual gets a full- time job. Just like with time, money management is a learned skill and is better understood with accountability. Teaching this practice begins with talking about it. As you discuss how your child will get money in college, you can begin to practice the process of receiving deposits, keeping a record of transactions, and understanding how a debit and credit card are different, and how each works. I believe it is a wise decision to teach them to avoid credit cards and learn to spend only what they have. If they can learn to manage a debit card now, they will keep themselves from the average $3000 debt in college. You might consider setting up a secret savings account with funds designated for overdraft until your teenager learns this practice. This way they may still have to pay a penalty, but they would not completely ruin themselves during the learning curve. As with most things, we often learn by making mistakes. We need to allow our kids to make those mistakes while protecting them from devastating consequences.

Questions

1. What do you think are going to be the most common struggles in time management with your college-bound child?

_____

_____

_____

_____

_____

_____

_____

2. What do you think are going to be the most common struggles in money management with your college-bound child?

_____

_____

_____

_____

_____

_____

3. What are some of the more practical life management issues that you will need to address with your child before college?

_____

_____

_____

_____

_____

_____

_____

_____

4. How will you put these new management traits into
   practice this year (make a list)?

_____

_____

_____

_____

_____

_____

5. What are some of the key points from this chapter that
   you will need to remember?

_____

_____

_____

_____

_____

_____

Chapter 6
Social Behaviors

As I have stated, college is a very social place. Everything about college is socially oriented. A student lives with his friends, studies with his friends, and shares downtime (which happens a lot in college) with his friends. The perception of a student's identity in college is found in the group she is connected to, the team he plays on, and the office she serves in a student organization. College is a society that thrives on community.

In high school, your son or daughter has probably been involved in many social groups as well. There are school clubs and teams, church groups, Christian organizations, and neighborhood clans. One might assume that a healthy social life in high school will equal a healthy social life in college, but that is not necessarily true. The difference in the two is accountability.

We have all seen the movies and know very well the image as pop culture has defined the stereotypes of college over the past few decades. From *Animal House* and *Revenge of the Nerds* to *American Pie* and *Old School*, college has been viewed on screen as one big party. Though often exaggerated, these college party stereotypes are real as that perspective has given generations of college students permission to join in on a lifestyle that lives up to that expectation.

This does not mean that teenagers will automatically fall into this life of nightly drinking, open drug use, and first date sleepovers, but they will certainly be in the vicinity of this behavior with the option to participate. This is why there needs to be a Social Behavior component to the Freedom Permit. Just because a teenager acts one way in high school will not guarantee that he will continue to behave the same way in college.

It Shouldn't Be About Morals
One of the big mistakes that a parent can make when dealing with social behaviors is to hang it on the mantle of being morally good. A desire to be a good boy or a good girl is a standard without boarders. A 12 year-old Christian female wants to be morally good after she hears a talk on purity at church and vows to wear a ring as a symbol. When she falls in love at the age of 17 to a boy who promises her the world, the ring comes off along with the moral stand. Committing to a moral behavior is a weak defense to the pressures of our society. Students who go off to college with this expectation will often crumble quickly.

Instead of basing behavior on looking and acting good morally, we should teach our kids to be faithful and pure because that is who God called us to be. If every believer is called to be the light of the world (Matthew 5), then this should include how we act in public and private places. Therefore, once you begin the process of Spiritual Development, discussions of social behavior could be close behind. 2 Timothy 2:15 says, "Do your best to present yourself to God as one approved, a worker who does not need to be ashamed and who correctly handles the word of truth." Colossians 3:17 says, "And whatever you do, whether in word or deed, do it all in the name of the Lord Jesus, giving thanks to God the Father through him." These verses remind us how to act as well as why we should act in such a way. We belong to God, as His children. We have been approved by God; and therefore, any other approval by anyone else is unnecessary.

Therefore, whatever we do, we should do because of whose we are and not how we want others to perceive us. As Philippians 4:8 reminds us, "Whatever is true, whatever is noble, whatever is right, whatever is pure, whatever is lovely, whatever is admirable--if anything is excellent or praiseworthy--think about such things." This is how we should behave. But how? How do we help anyone learn to live in such purity? Philippians 4:6-7 helps us answer that question: "Do not be anxious about anything, but in every situation, by prayer and petition, with thanksgiving, present your requests to God. And the peace of God, which transcends all understanding, will guard your hearts and your minds in Christ Jesus." We are unable to maintain a life of good morals because that is a standard based on our own power. Instead, let the "peace of God, which transcends all understanding, guard your hearts and your minds in Christ Jesus." He is our power, and this distinction should be taught to students before they pack up a broken moral compass expecting it to guide them throughout life.

Working The Plan
When thinking about teaching Christian teenagers how to act socially in college, one might focus solely on sex, drugs, and rock-n-roll, but we should go deeper into answering the why and help them connect their lifestyle choices to their identity and calling in Christ.

Social Behavior Conversations:
Conversations about social behaviors should be tied to Scripture and how the student thinks God wants them to live.

This will in fact create other social problems for the student who refuses to do certain things and act certain ways. By refusing to be one of the crowd, he may lose friends or miss out on times together. The student that takes this stand needs to know this is going to happen and needs to see that as a worthy consequence. There are a number of important conversations that need to take place regarding behaviors. The top three topics I believe are drug/alcohol use, sex and dating, and social media. Each of these is relevant to the world your child will be entering after this summer.

Chemical Substances - When it comes to things like alcohol and drugs, parents and kids find themselves all over the map of acceptance and understanding. Many parents send their child to college expecting them to get wasted every week, just like they once did. I say a lot about this in chapter 6 of my book *Lost in Transition*. Personally, I believe it is a matter of a believer's witness, based on 1 Corinthians 8. Because the subject is so taboo, I will allow you to approach it the way you think you need to. Keep in mind that it is a very important topic that must be addressed with your child so that he knows your feelings and expectations.

Sex and Dating - Dating in college is a completely different enterprise than in high school. The rules are different, the expectations are different, and the ethics of it are different as well. Here is a little nugget that you can share with your student when the time is right. I would remind them that practically everyone is someone's future spouse. That person they are dating may be someone else's future spouse, or he might be theirs, but not yet. Therefore, dating couples should treat each other like they are dating someone else's future spouse, knowing that someone may be currently dating their future spouse as well. That helps bring about a level of perspective that may not have been there before.

Social *Media* - Social media is not going away. Once

thought to be a fad, it has ushered in a new way of relating and communicating with others. Kids today are very savvy when it comes to social media and yet still a little naive to the dangers of it. I have known college kids to not get jobs because of online profiles, pictures, and statements. Girls have gotten kicked out of sororities, and boys have been put in jail. In the moment, social media postings seem fun and carefree, but they linger and can come back to bite you. Having a conversation about responsible social media behaviors is critical. If you do not feel qualified to have such a conversation, find someone who is. Spend some time researching the problems and discuss them with your kids.

Social Behavior Studies:
For this category, let me reiterate the need to research topics of concern so that you can be well informed when you have conversations with your kids.

Social Behavior Action:
One way to help your child through taking action is to have them develop a list of social non-negotiables before starting college. In my article, "Preparing For Liftoff," found in the Student Resource Library, I give students five things to do before moving to college.

One of those things is to develop a list of non-negotiables. A non-negotiable is some- thing that, under no circumstance, would you ever think about doing. It is a last-stand commitment you have with yourself. One example of a college related non-negotiable might be to never show up on test day without studying, never get drunk, or never be alone in a dorm room with someone of the opposite sex. These things can serve as guardrails to help keep your child focused and possibly prevent them from falling into a trap that they can't get out of. Once the list is made, the student should find someone to help keep him/her accountable for the non-negotiable list that has been made.

Questions

1. What do you need to tell your child about alcohol and drugs before college?

_____

_____

_____

_____

_____

_____

_____

2. What do you need to tell your child about sex and dating before college?

_____

_____

_____

_____

_____

_____

3. What do you need to tell your child about the dangers of social media to college students?

_____

_____

_____

_____

_____

_____

_____

4. How do you feel about having these conversations this year and what might you do to prepare for them?

_____

_____

_____

_____

_____

_____

_____

5. What are some of the key points from this chapter that you will need to remember?

_____

_____

_____

_____

_____

_____

_____

_____

Chapter 6
Goal Setting

The final category for the Freedom Permit is Goal Setting. Most teenagers are familiar with the concept of setting and reaching goals, but very few of them have actually had to do it in a major way. A student might set a goal for good grades or a high school athlete might actually set a goal for scoring a goal, but it is usually not until someone is on his own that his decisions come with major consequences. It takes discipline to reach goals, a quality that most teenagers do not yet possess fully. Helping your teenager understand how to set and reach goals is an important trait for someone who will soon be blazing new trails towards a career, life long relationships, and a life with many possibilities.

Setting goals is not rocket science, in theory. Simply put, you decide what you want to do, plan out the steps it takes to get there, and begin the process towards that destination. Yet, like many things, saying it and doing it are two completely different. So many times an individual plots a vision of his future, plunges forward to that target, only to find that he never wanted that goal in the first place. We see this in students who change majors multiple times in a four year span of college, and we see it in adults who jump from career to career, marriage to marriage, and opportunity to opportunity because they, like the classic song says, still haven't found what they are looking for.

There is a critical first step to goal setting that is often overlooked by followers of Christ. Just because an individual has a dream to reach a goal, that doesn't mean that this goal is to be reached. As believers, we have the God of the universe, creator of all things, guiding us to the life we were created to live. We have a navigator who is all powerful and all-knowing, yet so many times, we see a prize, look in to the direction of that opportunity, and dedicate ourselves in reaching a goal that we were never meant to reach. Proverbs 19:21 says, "Many are the plans in the mind of a man, but it is the purpose of the Lord that will stand." Proverbs 16:9 tell us, "The heart of man plans his way, but the Lord establishes his steps." As we teach our children how to set and reach goals, we must not forget the very first step of goal setting: determining God's goal for our life at that moment and making His goal, our goal. We must connect the dots from spiritual growth and development to the goal setting process as we prepare our kids for the challenges of life after high school.

The Fundamentals of Goal Setting
There are three basic fundamentals of learning the art of goal setting. As you spend this year preparing your child to make wise decisions and plan for his/her future, effective goal setting will be a critical skill to develop.

The first step in goal setting is understanding what it is that we want to accomplish. Again, this is where prayer is so important as we seek God's direction and plan. To an impatient, immature believer (which we all are at times) this seems like a waste of time. At first we might forget to include God in the planning stage of goal setting, and then when we do eventually remember, so much time has elapsed that we feel like we need to rush God's decision. Yet, as it says in Ephesians 3:20, God is the one "who is able to do immeasurably more than all we ask or imagine, according to his power that is at work within us." Waiting on God will mean that we start out with the right goal and will actually save you time in the end.

The second step in goal setting is creating a realistic, viable goal. Even though an individual might want to loose 50 pounds within the next week, that is not a realistic goal. Setting a goal to lose 5 pounds in a week and 50 pounds over the next year, though still aggressive, might be realistic. When setting a realistic goal, one must evaluate their gifts and talents, drive and determination, and timing and ability to perform. If an individual has the goal of losing weight, yet is not willing to exercise and change eating habits, then there is no will for the way. Goals need to be specific, clear, and attainable. This means that they need to be measurable and include a starting and ending point. The truth is, a goal without specifics is just a dream.

The third step in the process is to develop actionable steps to accomplish the goal. The goal setter will need to identify the obstacles and lay out the necessary "mini-goals" that need to be reached in order to get closer to the main goal. For example, if a college student wants to pursue a career in accounting, she will need to first look at the necessary course work, evaluate if her skill set fits this challenge, and then look at how many mini-goals must be reached in the process. One mini-goal might be to complete the pre-requisites necessary to get into the accounting program. Another secondary goal will be to do the needed work to sit for the CPA exam. Further mini-goals might be to prepare for the interview process, decide the type of accounting that this person would want to practice, and begin applying for those types of positions. Simply wanting to be an accountant is not good enough. A well thought out process is needed to reach that goal, all beginning with searching the Lord for the assurance that accounting is a vocational goal of this person's life.

Working The Plan

Just like the other steps in this year-long discipling pursuit, teaching goal setting works within the same three parameters: Goal Setting Conversations, Goal Setting Studies, and Goal Setting Actions.

Goal Setting Conversations:
Begin this process by asking questions about your teenager's dreams and desires. Start with the immediate possible goals (example: groups to join in college) and then move to other goals like majors, careers, etc. The more that your child can vocalize his/her hopes, the more clear they will begin to sound. Sometimes we just need to hear ourselves say these things out loud before they grow arms, legs, and begin to come alive. Have them talk about goals in four categories: spiritual growth (how will they grow deeper in Christ), community (relationships and groups), career (current and future jobs, school major and classes), and personal achievements (dreams, hobbies, travel, benchmarks). I suggest, at least at first, to let your child dream out loud. Resist the temptation to butt-in with comments of how unrealistic his ideas are or how her goals don't match her gift set. Let them dream and pray with them about their future and for God to reveal his purposes to your child. Having these conversations throughout the year could be monumental to your student's outlook on his/her journey ahead.

Goal Setting Studies:
This part might not be as critical for this category unless your child is extremely interested in developing the skill of goal setting. If this is the case, have them read a book or some articles on the subject and develop the most efficient process of setting and reaching goals for their personality.

Goal Setting Actions:

This is the stage when dreams begin to come together to make active goals. Before your child moves to college, I hope that you will take the opportunity to have them write out some of the goals that you have talked about. Writing out goals seems insignificant to some, but just like speaking them out loud, writing out a goal makes it seem real and identifiable. Below is a six-step exercise that I have laid out for students at the beginning of a new year in an article called "Planning For A Great Year!" in the Student Resource Library. This particular goal exercise is to help students develop goals for growing spiritually in the next year. You might start with this exercise before moving on to the other suggested goal categories.

1. Take out a piece of paper or find a blank sheet in a notebook or journal and answer these questions:
2. What was my walk with Christ like last year?
3. What were the moments of growth and struggle last year?
4. If I could do anything this year to mature in my faith, what would I do?
5. Share your answers with a friend who will keep you accountable for them.
6. Keep this list close to you and review and pray over it often.

You will see that this exercise starts by establishing the need for a goal. Looking back on last year, everyone can find ways to improve and grow when it comes to faith maturity. Then, this is followed by a question of how the student would like to improve in the next year. This leads him/her in writing those ideas down, turning them into goals and then sharing those goals with someone for accountability.

Allow this process of discovery to energize you and your child as you dream together, talking about how you see his gifts, and fleshing out those ideas into functional, manageable goals for college. Help him to see that this process is necessary to focus clearly on his journey of living the life that he is called to live. Once an individual has a clear vision for who he is and what he has been called to do/be, he will be excited to continue living the life that he was created to live.

Questions

1. How has your child shown good goal setting skills in the past?

_____

_____

_____

_____

_____

_____

_____

2. What specific goals do you think you will need to focus on with your child this year?

_____

_____

_____

_____

_____

_____

_____

_____

3. What success have you personally had with goal
   setting in the past and how could you use that
   experience to help your student?

_____

_____

_____

_____

_____

_____

4. What ways, if any, do think you will be able to help
   your child stay on track with these goals after the
   transition to college?

_____

_____

_____

_____

_____

_____

_____

_____

5. What are some of the key points from this chapter that
   you will need to remember?

_____

_____

_____

_____

_____

_____

_____

Chapter 7
TheTransMission

In 2010, after over 16 years of active youth ministry, I founded TheTransMission which is a ministry that seeks to guide, protect, and develop the faith of young followers of Christ, during their transition from high school to college, so that they can live and lead as the light of the world. This organization works with churches, schools, and families to help guide graduating students to reach five core goals by the end of their first college semester. These five core goals are:

CONFIDENT in who they are in Christ

ORIENTED in their new surroundings

RESPONSIBLE for their schedule and decisions

ENGAGED in serving and growing in their walk with Christ through ministry

SURROUNDED by friends in Christ-like community

CONFIDENT in who they are in Christ
Identity is so important for any follower of Christ at any age, but for college freshmen, it is the one key ingredient to how

well they transition spiritually to college. The reason for this is two-fold. First, college students are at an age where they are trying to answer the questions: "Who am I?" and "Who do I want to be?" This season of self-discovery can either help a young Christian become confident in who he has been created to be, or it can be the beginning of years (maybe decades) of identity struggles. Secondly, the culture of college is a battleground for one's identity, no matter how strong and sure they are in their faith. Reaching this goal early in college will save a student from many struggles and hardships to come.

ORIENTED in their new surroundings
Prior to moving off to college, a student has been living in a safe home environment with guidelines and rules to live by. As college students, not only are they on their own, away from Mom and Dad, but they must navigate through day to day life by themselves. The sooner freshmen can become familiar with their new surroundings, the more comfortable they will feel in college. This will ease any stress or homesickness that might take place.

RESPONSIBLE for their schedule and decisions
One of the key characteristics of adulthood is responsibility. A college student who is responsible for her schedule and decisions is one that will make the most of her college experience.

ENGAGED in serving and growing in their walk with Christ through ministry
The only way that a follower of Christ is going to continue to mature in her faith is to become connected to ministry opportunities to serve and be discipled. Jesus was clear that we are to serve others, and that this act of service is how we demonstrate our love for Him. College campuses are loaded with these types of opportunities, and the sooner a student can plug into them, the better.

<u>SURROUNDED by friends in Christ-like community</u>
College is a social society and most freshmen will want to surround themselves with new friends and groups to be a part of. These groups that allow them to connect to other students will begin to mold them into a reflection of the ideas, morals, and conduct of the group. If a Christ-follower is committed to growing in his faith, he will need to surround himself with others who have the same interests and desires. This will be important for accountability, growth, and fellowship.

Understanding A Transition Year

TheTransMission operates on what I call a Transition Year. A Transition Year, or Trans Year for short, is the calendar year of a student's graduation. This 12-month period represents the student's last semester of high school and first semester of college. This is the season that the student is most focused on the transition and most active in the process of transitioning. The content in the Student Resource Library helps students prepare to be spiritually responsible for their maturity, decisions, relationships, and future. The Library includes a monthly checklist for the student, beginning in January of the senior year and continuing until the end of the freshman year of college.

TheTransMission Resources

TheTransMission has created transition-related resources for everyone involved in the process of a student's transition. This book, for example, is a way to help parents lead the process during a student's senior year. For parents with a few more years before starting this journey, I recommend *Ownership Road: Leading Our Children To An Authentic Faith That Prepares Them For Life After High School.* For students, the main resource is my book *Lost in Transition: Becoming Spiritually Prepared for College.* This book, in its second edition, helps a high school senior or college freshman understand the challenges of faith in college and how to grow in that new setting. There is more on *Lost in Transition* on the ministry website. Other resources like *Own Your Own*, an online video series that teaches the content of *Lost in Transition* in five sessions, is also available. For ministry leaders, an online audio course called *Bridging The Gap* is available for download. More resources are always in development and might not be listed here.

A Good List To Start With
In conclusion, I wanted to give you a list of 12 things that parents can do before their student graduates and moves on to college. Many of these suggestions will act as a summary of the material that has been presented in this book. My prayer is that you will take this all in and be able to relay it to your high school seniors, so that they can move away from home with all the confidence and vision they will need to make a healthy and smooth transition, not only to college, but in life.

12 Things A Parent Of A Senior Should Do Before (or just after) Graduation Day

1. *Be sure your children know how proud you are of them.* Actions don't always speak louder than words. They might be too distracted to notice your actions, but they need to know how you feel. It is important to their self-confidence that they know that they have your support. Celebrate them & their accomplishments.

2. *Begin to give them a little more freedom than you have before.* They will have full freedoms in college, and your offering to give them a little more freedom at home now will communicate to them that you understand their desires.

3. *Spend time having fun together.* Going on a trip together, having a fun night out, or a family game night at home will develop your family relationship and give you time to spend with your child before she goes off to college. Give them great memories of family time.

4. *Have a talk about money and time management.* As I have already stated, most college freshmen do not know how to manage money or time. They need to practice this before moving to college and hear helpful advice for mastering both managing principles.

5. *Have a talk about relationships.* Many students don't go into college fully understanding that the people they meet and form friendships with will dictate who they become and how they are perceived by others. They need to be wise about who they begin to develop relationships with.

6. *Ask them about their goals, dreams, & plans.* If this doesn't sound like a normal conversation to have with your child, then you are in a relational deficit. Two reasons this is important: one, asking them to share makes them think about their future and, secondly, it shows them that you care and are interested in them.

7. *Be quick to listen and slow to speak.* Most teenagers don't think that their parents understand them. They often feel that parents just want to instruct them, which makes them feel more like a child than a young adult. Ask questions and then listen. Resist the urge to always put in your "two cents" and wait to offer advice until they ask for it.

8. *Tell them about your college experience.* Be careful not to just tell a bunch of party stories without sharing the lessons that you have learned. Don't be afraid to share with them some of your struggles and successes. Let them know that you were actually in their shoes once

and that you understand what they are going through.

9. *Encourage them to stay connected to their mentors.*
There is no doubt that your child has had ministry leaders, teachers and coaches who have impacted him in his growth and walk with Christ during his years in high school. Encourage him to stay connected to these influences throughout the summer and even while in college. Everyone needs mentors in their life, and until your child replaces those relationships, there will be a void.

10. *Talk out the specifics.* Because your child has never lived on her own before, she is not accustomed to thinking about all of the specific details that independence will involve. You know these things because of experience and wisdom. Share that wisdom with her as you talk out the details that she may not have thought of yet.

11. *Ask them for advice.* This one may sound strange, but if you are going to trust your college student to be away on his own, you should trust his opinion as well. Think of something that you need his advice on and ask. One, it will assure him that you see him as a young adult, and two, you might actually learn something.

12. *Pray with them and for them.* Nothing will tell your child that you care more than to sit him down and pray over him. If this is not natural for your family, then do it often enough so that it begins to feel more normal. Let your child know that you will continue to pray for him daily while he is in college.

ABOUT THE AUTHOR

Tommy McGregor is an author, speaker, ministry coach/consultant, and the founder of TheTransMission, a ministry devoted to guiding kids through to a healthy spiritual transition of life after high school. Tommy has spent over two decades in ministry working with students, parents, and mentors, and is passionate about helping others develop a sense of who God has created them to be. He lives in Montgomery, AL with his wife Andrea and their two boys, Webb and Wolf. Tommy can be contacted directly at tommy@tommymcgregor.com, as well as on Twitter at @tommymcgregor.

Other Books by Tommy McGregor

Lost in Transition: Becoming Spiritually Prepared For College, second edition 2012, Tate Publishing

Selfie: A Parent's Guide To Social Media, 2015, TDR Publishing

Ownership Road: Leading Our Children To An Authentic Faith That Prepares Them For Life After High School, 2016, TDR Publishing

Made in the USA
Columbia, SC
22 September 2020

21124488R00037